# spot

## AFRICAN ANIMALS

# GIRAFFES

by Mary Ellen Klukow

AMICUS | AMICUS INK

# horns

# neck

Look for these
words and pictures
as you read.

# spots

# tongue

Look! What is behind that tree?
It is a giraffe!

The giraffe is the tallest
animal on land.
A giraffe can be 18 feet (5.5 m) tall.

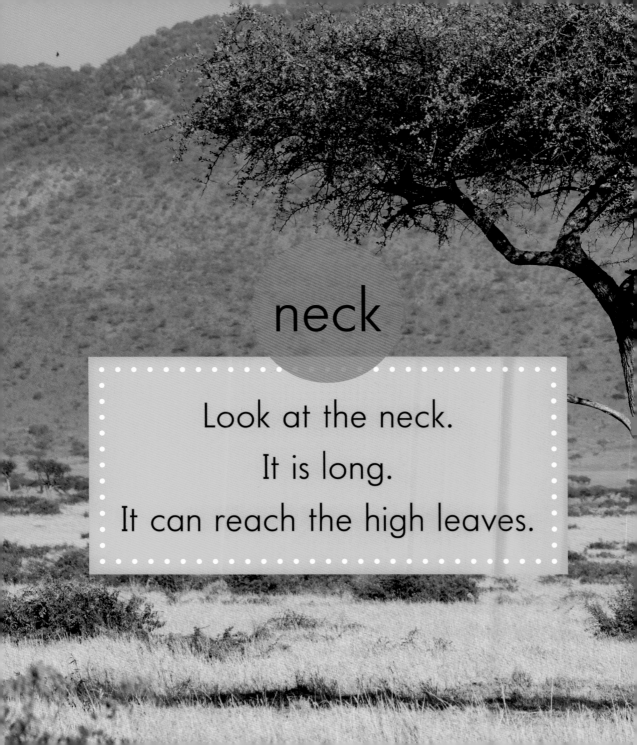

# neck

Look at the neck.

It is long.

It can reach the high leaves.

**horns**

Look at the horns.
Males and females both have horns.
Males use them to fight.

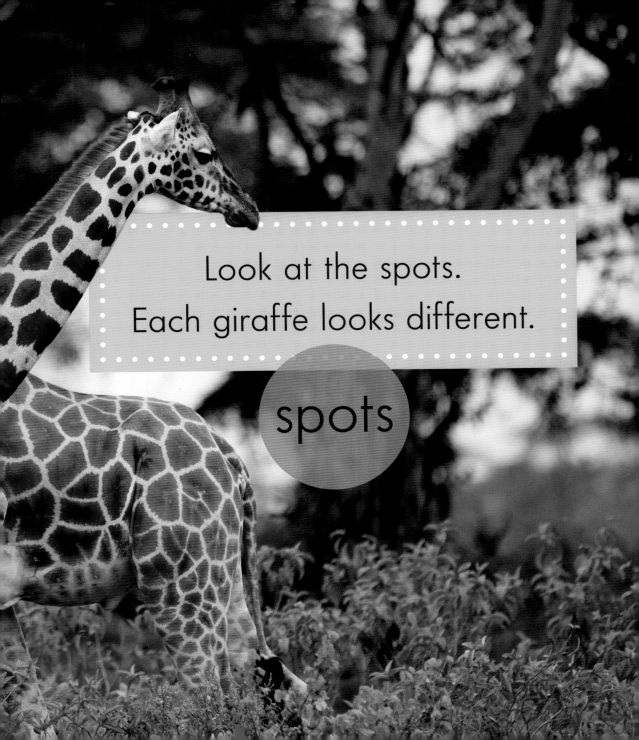

Look at the spots.
Each giraffe looks different.

spots

# tongue

Look at the tongue.
It is tough.
Thorns don't hurt it.

A baby giraffe runs.
She can walk one hour after birth.
She follows her mom.

## horns

## neck

Did you find?

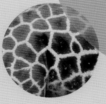

## spots

## tongue

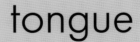

spot

Spot is published by Amicus and Amicus Ink
P.O. Box 1329, Mankato, MN 56002
www.amicuspublishing.us

Library of Congress Cataloging-in-Publication Data
Names: Klukow, Mary Ellen, author.
Title: Giraffes / by Mary Ellen Klukow.
Description: Mankato, Minnesota : Amicus, [2020] |
  Series: Spot. African animals | Audience: K to Grade 3.
Identifiers: LCCN 2018025776 (print) | LCCN 2018031228
  (ebook) | ISBN 9781681517216 (ebook) | ISBN
  9781681516394 (library binding) | ISBN 9781681524252
  (paperback)
Subjects:  LCSH: Giraffe--Africa--Juvenile literature.
Classification: LCC QL737.U56 (ebook) | LCC QL737.U56
  K58 2020 (print) | DDC 599.638--dc23
LC record available at https://lccn.loc.gov/2018025776

Printed in China

HC   10 9 8 7 6 5 4 3 2 1
PB   10 9 8 7 6 5 4 3 2 1

Wendy Dieker and Alissa Thielges, editors
Deb Miner, series designer
Ciara Beitlich, book designer
Holly Young, photo researcher

Photos by by Getty/Marc Rauw cover,
16; iStock/kotomiti 1; Shutterstock/
otografieKuhlmann 3; Shutterstock/
Volodymyr Burdiak 4–5; Minden/Denis-
Huot 6–7; iStock/GlobalP 8–9, 12–13;
iStock/Palenque 10–11; Minden/Suzi
Eszterhas 14

GIRAFFES